D1076495

Tina Turner
the best of
simply the best

Wise Publications
London / New York / Sydney

Exclusive Distributors:
Music Sales Limited
8/9 Frith Street, London W1V 5TZ, England.
Music Sales Pty Limited
120 Rothschild Avenue, Rosebery, NSW 2018, Australia.

This book © Copyright 1992 by Wise Publications.
Order No.AM88310
ISBN 0-7119-2939-4

New arrangements by Roger Day.
Photographs courtesy of Lorraine Day KATZ Pictures: p.3.
London Features Limited: p.4/5/6.

Music Sales' complete catalogue lists thousands of titles and is
free from your local music shop, or direct from Music Sales Limited.
Please send a cheque/postal order for £1.50 for postage to:
Music Sales Limited, Newmarket Road, Bury St. Edmunds, Suffolk IP33 3YB.

Printed in the United Kingdom by
J.B. Offset Printers (Marks Tey) Limited, Marks Tey, Essex.

Addicted To Love   50

Break Every Rule   60

I Can't Stand The Rain   18

It Takes Two   44

Let's Stay Together   21

Private Dancer   34

River Deep - Mountain High   39

Steamy Windows   24

The Best   7

Way Of The World   56

We Don't Need Another Hero   30

What's Love Got To Do With It   12

The Best

Words & Music by Mike Chapman / Holly Knight

Moderate rock

(1.) I call you, I need you, my heart's on fire. _____
(Verses 2 & 3 see block lyric)

You come to me, come to me,

wild and wired._____ Oh you come to me,

give me ev-'ry-thing I ___ need. (2.) Give me a

2. You're sim-ply the best, ___ bet-ter than

all ___ the rest, ___ bet-ter than a - ny-one, ___ a-ny-one I've

VERSE 2:
Give me a lifetime of promises, and a world of dreams
Speak the language of love like you know what it means
Mm, and it can't be wrong
Take my heart and make it strong babe.

VERSE 3:
In your heart, in the stars, every night and every day
In your eyes I get lost, I get washed away
Just as long as I'm here in your arms
I could be in no better place.

What's Love Got To Do With It

Words & Music by Graham Lyle / Terry Britten

VERSE

must un - der - stand ___ that the touch of ___ your hand ___ makes my

pulse re - act; ___ that it's on - ly ___ the thrill ___ of

boy meet - ing girl; ___ op - po - sites at - tract. ___ It's

phys - i - cal, on - ly log - i - cal, ___

Verse 2:
It may seem to you
That I'm acting confused
When you're close to me.
If I tend to look dazed,
I read it some place;
I've got cause to be.
There's a name for it,
There's a phrase that fits,
But whatever the reason,
You do it for me.

(To Chorus)

I Can't Stand The Rain

Words & Music by Don Bryany / Ann Peebles / Bernard Miller

VERSES

When we was to-geth - er____
Wo - o emp - ty pil - low____

G   F

ev - 'ry-thing___ was so grand,   Now that we've par-
where his head___ used to lay,___   I___ know you got___

G   Bb

ted___   there's just   one sound   that I just___
___ some sweet___ mem-or-ies, but like the win - dow   you ain't got

Am7

1.   2.
___ can't___ stand___ I can't stand the rain___   noth - ing to say___ I can't stand the rain_

D7   D7

19

CHORUS

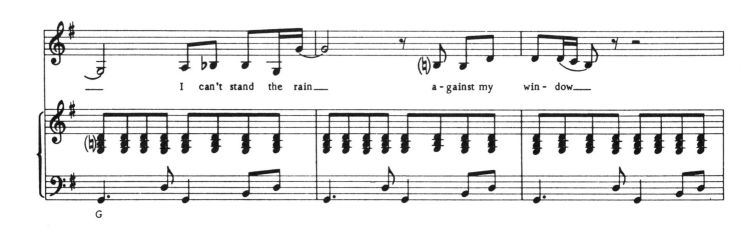

Repeat and fade 2nd time

20

Let's Stay Together

Words & Music by Willie Mitchell / Al Green / Al Jackson

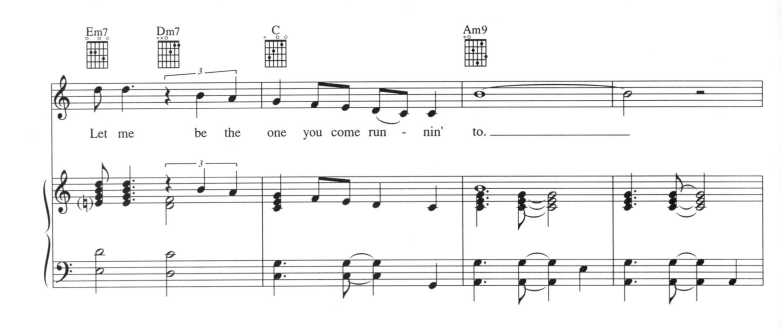

Let me be the one you come run - nin' to. _____

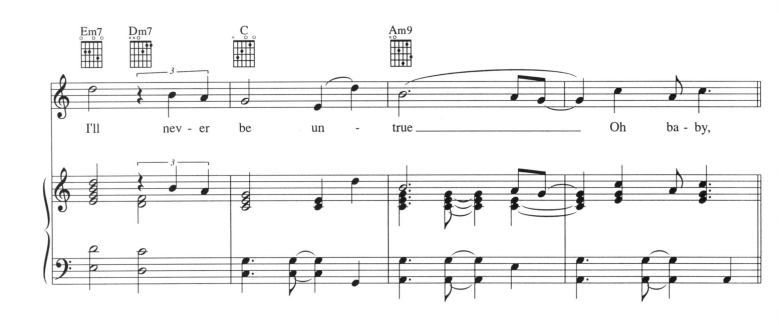

I'll nev - er be un - true _____ Oh ba - by,

CHORUS

let's, _____ let's stay to - geth - er,

1st time in tempo
3rd time instrumental

Verse 3:
Why, tell me,
Why do people break up
And turn around and make up?
I just can't see.
You'd never do that to me;
Just being around you is all I see. So baby,

(To chorus)

Steamy Windows

Words & Music by Tony Joe White

(1.) I was think - in' 'bout park - ing the oth - er night

we was out on the back row.

Me and my ba - by was just get - ting right, ___ all sys -tems go, o - ver -load. ___

Ra - di - o blast -ing in the

front seat, turn -ing out the mu - sic fine. ___

And we were snug-gled up in the back seat,

com -ing from the bo - dy heat. ___

To Coda

VERSE 2:
You can wine and dine with a man all night
With good intent
But there's something about a confrontation on the back row
Breaks down the defence.

VERSE 3:
There's a sound outside the front door
And I know it's just the wind
But it makes them snuggle up just a little bit closer
And starts things happening again.

CHORUS on D.S.
Steamy windows
It ain't nobody can see
Steamy windows
Coming from the body heat
Steamy windows
Zero visibility
Steamy windows
Coming from body heat.

Steamy windows . . .

We Don't Need Another Hero

Words & Music by Graham Lyle / Terry Britten

Verse 2:
Looking for something we can rely on
There's got to be something better out there.
Love and compassion, their day is coming,
All else are castles built in the air.

Private Dancer

Words & Music by Mark Knopfler

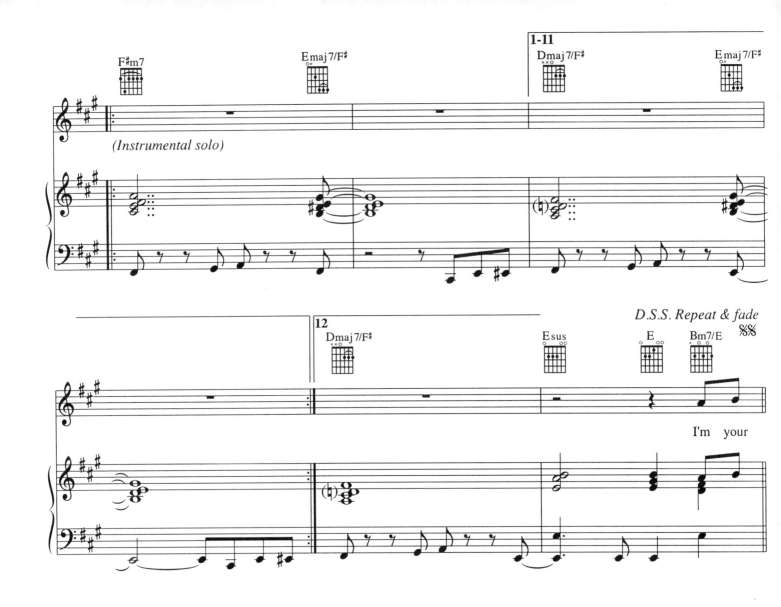

Verse 2:
You don't think of them as human.
You don't think of them at all.
You keep your mind on the money,
Keeping your eyes on the wall.

(To Chorus:)

Verse 3:
I want to make a million dollars.
I want to live out by the sea.
Have a husband and some children;
Yeah, I guess I want a family.

River Deep - Mountain High

Words & Music by Phil Spector / Ellie Greenwich / Jeff Barry

-er,—   let me say,—   And it gets high-
-ger, ba - by,   and hea-ven knows,—   And it gets sweet-

-er—   day by day.—
-er, ba - by,   as it grows.—

Chorus

Do I love you, right or wrong?—————————————— Yeah

river — er deep, moun-tain high, — yeah yeah yeah. —

If I lost you, would I cry? —

I would, ba - by, — ba - by, — ba - by. —

fine

a tempo

When you were a young boy did —

42

It Takes Two

Words & Music by William Stevenson/Sylvia Moy

it takes two _____ ba - by, _____ just me and you.__

You know it takes two. __

Ad lib. to Fade

VERSE 2:

One can have a broken heart
Living in misery
Two can really ease the pain
Like a perfect remedy
One can be alone in a bar
Like an island he's all alone
Two can make just any place
Seem just like being at home.

VERSE 3:

One can go out to a movie
Looking for a special treat
Two can make that simple movie
Something really kinda neat
And one can take a walk in the moonlight
Thinking that it's really nice
But two lovers walking hand in hand
It's like adding just a pinch of spice.

Addicted To Love

Words & Music by Robert Palmer

The lights are

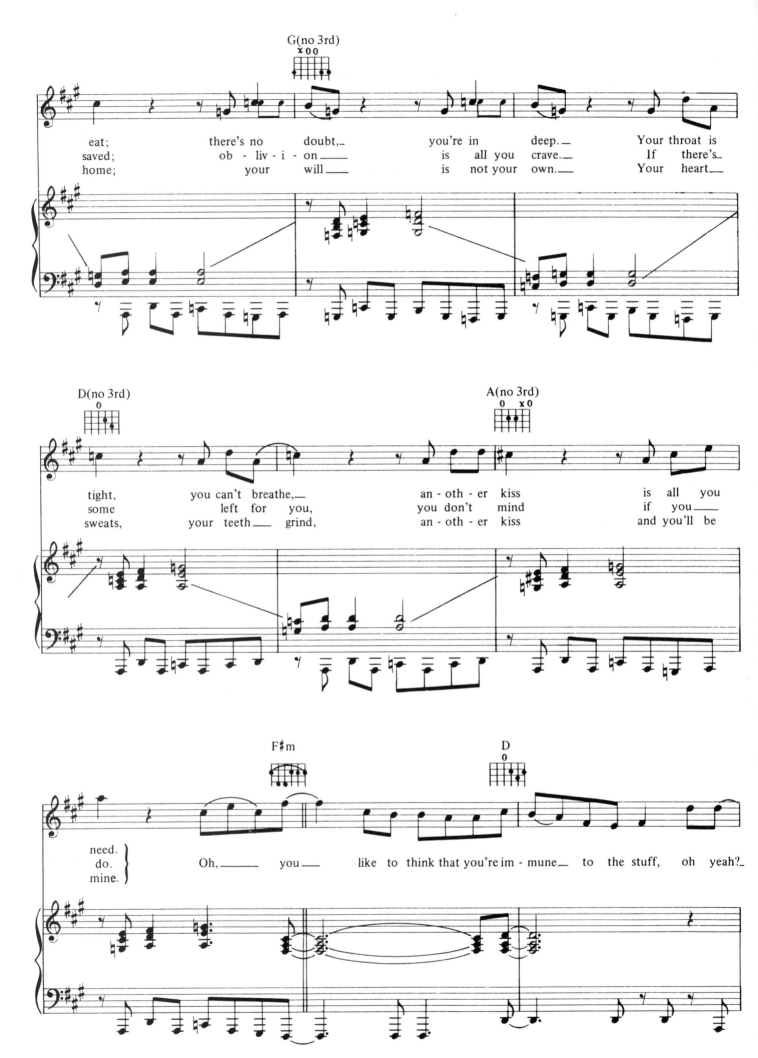

It's clos-er___ to the truth to say you

1.
can't get e-nough; you know you're gon-na have to face it; you're ad-dict-ed to love.___ You see the

2.
gon-na have to face it; you're ad-dict-ed to love.___ Might___ as well face it you're ad-

dict-ed to love.___ Might___ as well face it you're ad-dict-ed to love.___ Might___

Way Of The World

Words & Music by G. Lyle / A. Hammond

Verse 2: Baby, I will go anywhere you lead
As long as you're there beside me
Baby that's all I need
Hold me, hold me and never let me go
I'm always gonna care about you
I never wanna be without you.

Break Every Rule

Words & Music by Rupert Hine / Jeannette Obstoj

un-der your spell. ___ I've made my mis-takes, _ oh, ___ you can prob-ab-ly tell. ___

BRIDGE

You're ev-'ry dream that ___ I dream; ___

you're ev-'ry beau-ti-ful thing ___ I've ev-er seen. ___ I'm al-ways

sing-ing your prais-es, count-ing the days ___ a-way. ___

Verse 2:
I hope you can forgive
Every white lie that I'm forced to tell.
They say that everything's fair in love and in war,
And I'm not above cheating for you.
One night, I'll catch you off your guard,
And you will finally fall so hard.
Strategically speaking, I'm already beaten;
I'll surrender to you.

(To Bridge:)